T0198875

Moms Who Hate to Say "NO!"
and Workbook for Busy Moms

. . . .

Sue Balding

BALBOA
PRESS
A DIVISION OF HAY HOUSE

Balboa Press books may be ordered through booksellers or by contacting:

Balboa Press
A Division of Hay House
1663 Liberty Drive
Bloomington, IN 47403
www.balboapress.com
1-(877) 407-4847

ISBN: 978-1-4525-3650-7 (sc)
ISBN: 978-1-4525-3651-4 (e)

Cover Design by Bill Krueger

Printed in the United States of America

Balboa Press rev. date: 08/17/2011

To Geema with love and affection always.

Dear Reader,

This book comes from years of acquiring information from my children who have been my biggest teachers. I wrote it to share some insights that would be wasted if not put down on paper for another parent perhaps looking for some answers. I did not do everything "right" as a parent but I found I had collected many lessons from being a Mom.

Some lessons were hard to learn and some happened as time went on and I listened to what my children had to say. I did find that listening was the greatest gift I could give them and myself. To ask how to do it differently was a leading thought behind what you find here.

Sometimes just being unconventional was what worked best for my family. I'm sure you will be able to add to this small work to make it the best for you. There are no "perfect" answers. I do know that in searching for the best way to deal with parenting takes time, effort, consistency, patience, and a lot of love. In the end, it is all worth it.

This job of parenting is never-ending. I have learned also that the time to let go and let be does come at different ages for each child. They will come to you after they supposedly have grown up, for a tweak (or advice), when they need it and if the communication is given freely and not given until asked.

I have been lucky to have loved four wonderful human beings that have come to me through this life. They have made me a better person and continue to allow me to love more fully in all aspects of my journey here on this earth.

All of us as parents are blessed with gifts far beyond what we expected and have taken us to shores we may never have anticipated. I count my blessings that have appeared in many different forms; some of struggles, some with pure joy. I hope the best for you in your journey as a parent.

Blessings to you

Contents

1. Are You One of Them? 1

2. The Hardest and Most Rewarding Job You'll Ever Have. 9

3. The Nuts and Bolts of "Counting to 10". 15

4. Rules to Live By. 19

5. The Model of Human Functioning 25

6. The Mad Hatter's Tea Party 29

7. Does Your Teenager Look Like An Adult?. 33

8. Practice, Practice, Practice. 39

9. Teach How To "Be" Your Best, It's Better Than A's! 45

10. Workbook for Busy Moms 47

Chapter 1

. . . .

Are You One of Them?

I'm talking about the Moms who want to be "friends" with their children. That goes for Dads too. We seem to be falling into a misuse of parenting that socially is becoming acceptable, but we are not paying attention to the consequences.

When we as parents look to our children for validation, acceptance, love - coming to us from the outside; we are upside down and back to front. Our main support system in parenting needs to be coming from each other. Love of self comes first for any self confidence, which then translates into relationships as a partner, friends, family connections, and then once we have children; as a parent.

Are you concerned with what makes your child happy in the moment? What do material things do for us in the long run? Are you placing limits for your children? Disappointment can actually teach patience. Fits of a young child not getting what they want are not there for us to give in, but they are asking for guidance in the only language they know.

Are we listening? Can we teach limits? Yes! It doesn't have to just be the word "No!" The important part of parenting is often the explanation or the "why" behind the initial message. Are we teaching to that depth? It seems not at the moment. There is a better way.

It takes what I call conscious living and parenting. That is simply taking apart what we are doing and looking at it from a different point of view. Awareness begins the journey into change. We need to change it up to give our children the best possible chance at life. Everything is changing so fast today. Can we keep up as parents? I think we can.

Being a parent is the most challenging and rewarding job we can ever have. It's hard to be the one to draw the line for behavior of a child at any age. So when we choose to look at parenting from a material standpoint or what we have, wear, appear to the outside world; we are not going deep enough to give our children true stability that they can take away and use on their own journey beyond us.

What is the most important thing to us as parents? That our children are happy perhaps? What can bring that happiness to them in life? We are not guaranteed anything but the ground work on which you parent is ultimately what pays off. What they do with it in their life is their choice.

Parents are the teachers of what is right and wrong, acceptable and not acceptable behavior, values, principles, truth, spirituality, love.

In my life I have learned from raising four children that they teach us. I have collected those teachings into this book to help anyone else searching for basic ground rules as an encouragement that you can do this and do a great job. I've made many mistakes myself, but it's true, you learn from failure.

Giving everything to our children is not as easy today. Perhaps this is a good thing. Now we can concentrate on conscious parenting. By that I mean, giving our children guide lines to live by. Being aware of what we teach on a day-to-day basis means more from this point of view.

Everything we do and say – they are watching and replicating in one way or another. Our intention becomes paramount in parenting when we look at it from here.

Boundaries are important for children. They learn them only by the family contacts they have in their life; with parents, siblings, relatives. Early life teachings are like underpinnings to character.

When we as parents learn to say "No!" with love in our hearts, they hear and feel it. They may squawk and complain, but that just means it's working. Our discipline does not, however, have to be unkind, threatening, punishing, or stifling. Read on to find some helpful hints from a mom who has done it all different ways. I'd like to share some of my failures as well as successes.

Please take from it what best suits your family. Just remember, you are the bottom line. To be a parent is an awesome, inspiring, boundary setting job. Do your job with conviction and stick-to-it-ive-ness (together) and your gifts to your children will be immeasurable.

Quite honestly, I think we were conditioned into this belief that we just can't say "No!" Think about it. From the time our little wonders enter into this world we are told to listen to their cries and figure out what they mean. In rather short order actually you can attune yourself to what the "hunger" cry is; the "I'm wet and can't stand it anymore" cry; the "I'm not ready for my nap" cry; then there's the "if you don't put me down for a nap now, YOU are going to be sooo sorry" cry, etc.

This conditioning of tuning into our babies seems to build up over time. Some of us never really "get it," so don't think this book isn't for you too. I have a story I'd like to share with you with regard to some of us who don't "get it."

Shared story:

A friend of mine came over shortly after I was home with my firstborn child and she kidnapped me saying, "You haven't been out of this house since the hospital. Today we are going out for lunch." Robin (my husband) was baby sitting. I flung a quick "Here you go, Robin. We'll be back in two hours." And just like that we were off. I must admit I had a marvelous time just being on my own, with my friend.

Laughingly we arrived back to the house and as we were coming up to the back door I saw my husband standing outside on the porch with a frown on his face (more like terror, actually) jostling the baby who was crying bloody murder!

He said, "I've tried everything. I've changed his diaper, walked around for the last forty minutes, tried the pacifier, but he just spits that out. What on earth am I doing wrong?!" I said, "Well, honey, it is past 2pm, have you had lunch yet? No? Well neither has he. Did you try a bottle? I left one for you of breast milk, remember?" Robin said, "Oh, I wasn't hungry and I never even thought about that with him screaming like this. I'm so glad you're home – here."

It does take trial and error to figure out the different cries. Like the ones in the middle of the night, right? If you're nursing on demand you really have to wait to have a schedule figured out by both of you. You will produce more milk as the demand increases. Guess what, that means they cry more when they are hungry and you take the cue.

I called my grandmother over this once. "Grandma, what do I do when he seems to be wanting to eat every two hours?" She had so many helpful hints that I could write down so I'll share them with you. "He's helping you to produce more milk to allow him to grow. They don't come here with a Dr. Spock book attached to them. Sometimes even the digestive system isn't 100% yet. Don't get upset, because he will too. You have to learn to be the parent and calmly handle the situation."

Easier said than done? What choice do you have? Learning how to deal with our own issues is part of becoming a true parent. Our children from a very early age are our best teachers. So roll up your sleeves and come along with me for a Magic Bus Ride – a euphemism for the wild ride you are about to begin.

Now that you have totally recalculated your system to fit with your baby, change happens. No one told us that you can end up with a demanding, temper tantrumming, and unreasonable toddler. How do you think that happened? You probably didn't give up the "Mommy" persona that you thought was working (and it probably was, for that infant stage). The tough lesson that comes next is on the cover of this book and it lasts for the rest of your foreseeable future. It's called the "No!" stage, which is not just the one children go through because it's their NEW word and they are testing out their independence.

There are many ways to say the word "No" and mean it and several ways to say the word "No" without actually using it, a very good trick to learn for your "bag of tricks" as a mom.

We all get tired of repeating ourselves with this short, succinct, definitive sounding word. Who wants to sound like a broken record? Words are our defense mechanism that we must learn how to manipulate eloquently for our children. There are so many ways to say no, it's just that that one word is so quick to come into the mind. Follow along with another of my grandmother's words of wisdom and you'll discover many ways to say "No!"

Something I have learned over the years is that the more attention I put into the words I use (in any situation), the better my results, and the less agitated I become in aggravating scenarios. Read on and you will find out how to "Count to 10" and use it for the focus that you want for not saying just "No!"

The older our children become, the more they need to understand the meaning of the word "No." Our society has become one of instant gratification. It is our responsibility to model restraint and good thinking before acting (acquiring) and the benefits of that. No <u>thing</u> actually ever satisfies us for long. Do you find that to be true?

Basically, we constantly look outside ourselves for satisfaction in this human form and in this reality.

Actually, it's all found within. If we could teach our children that true fulfillment comes from inside of us, we could be on a great road to true prosperity.

When we tell our children, "Mommy can't get that for you today, sweetie, maybe next time." What do you think they actually are hearing? "Mommy WON'T buy me that right now and it's making me angry and I'm going to stomp around until she gives in and gets it!" Whatever happened to, "Mommy isn't going to buy toys today. We came here for groceries so you can help me make those mashed potatoes that you love, remember?" How difficult was that? You had to *think* about that one?

Take any scenario you can and apply thinking differently and see how you do. See? You can do it. You can make a difference in your life and in that of your child. AND, what did it cost you? Time. What do you have at this exact moment?

Moms think we have to give whatever is going to make our children happy so that they grow up to BE happy. Isn't that what we all want, a better world for our children, with happiness abounding. How does one achieve happiness?

Does it come from the "toys" that we buy (bigger toys for bigger boys scenario). Maybe for an instant, but then isn't it a moving target? You know that next week it will be something else, and then something else, and then something else. Let's instead focus on what we HAVE. Now there's a new idea.

If we live from a place of gratitude we can get there. Our children are watching everything we do in life. They learn from what we do, not necessarily from what we say. *"Do as I say, not as I do!"* Silly saying, isn't it? But that is what the majority of us do. So try practicing gratitude instead by speaking about how lucky you are with what you already have: healthy, thriving children who test your limits, but love you unconditionally; a home filled with love for all who enter, even Aunt Dottie who tries everyone's patience, but boy do we have some funny stories! We must count our gratitudes each and every day. Focus on the positive and believe me, you will create more of it.

In order to BE a parent you cannot be a FRIEND. I know this is disappointing to many. Your job that you signed up for when you gave birth and welcomed this little bundle into your lives was more life challenging than you bargained for, thought of, or even realized. But you do want to be a "friend," confidante and have them come to you for help and advice don't you?

The interesting truth of the matter is that the parent role encompasses being strict and setting limits (teaching boundaries in many more ways than you could imagine). In other words, sometimes being the "bad guy." That bad guy is more important than any friend. In fact, it's not the bad guy, it's the smart life-lesson guy that they NEED.

When we remain friends with our children because it is easier when they are young, the teen years will test you beyond belief. If you don't figure out how to *lovingly* be the disciplinarian (both of you as parents) at an early age of your child, it only gets tougher (for you).

We all love our children and want them to be happy. Looking at the whole parenting time of my life from this vantage point I can see what I'm about to tell you clearly. I know you will probably have a hard time listening to it, but I can only challenge you to try out some of the following tactics and see for yourself.

The outcome of not being the true parent to your children is consequences beyond my explanation and unforeseeable by you. It takes trust to believe in what I say. I can only hope that you try some things out for yourself and realize that the results may even take years to come to fruition. You will be glad in the end that you did hear this message.

We want only the very best for our children. But *giving* them everything plus the things we wanted when we were young (a potentially huge backfire) is not what they need. What they need is not in things. It is not tagible in the material. Our selves is the most valued gift to our children. Our time being with them; our guidance in what is right and wrong; our values of character; our boundaries to keep them safe; our wisdom from living.

Especially in times like today we have opportunities presenting themselves to parent better. The material is not as readily available to us. Thank goodness! We all have to cut back. Now the questions can be; how do I tell my child No and not hurt him (or is it, have him mad with me?). How did I suddenly become that parent I never wanted to be? The answer is relatively simple and simple is what we all need, especially as parents. There is an effective way to inform children about what's up for us all in the real world: TELL THE TRUTH.

Yes, it's that simple. At all ages our children learn from us by our actions. Communication, communication, communication is the mantra for all relationships – even with our children. You will be amazed by what they can understand. Give them the chance to show you how resilient they can be. Get them involved in "how" to save in these unpredictable, hard times. I like to look at it as an *opportunity* to grow as a family and come together.

Later in this book you'll find out how to have a Family Meeting. Here is where your nuts and bolts of communication can occur. Speak your truth about the family's situation. Speak of how we all have to pull together to make this work, with whatever we **have.** Count our gratitudes together and work to be a great team against all odds. We CAN make it and even make it better than before.

Ask your children for their ideas of what would help. Give them opportunities to be engaged and to *think* of solutions too. You will be amazed at their curiosity, creativity and then willingness to do what's needed.

When we give responsibility to our children and then let go, they are able to make their own mistakes, learn from them, and grow into strong and responsible people. Let's face it; life hasn't been all happiness for us, has it? Why do we expect to be able to keep struggles from them? It's not what life is all about.

So let's unconditionally love our children, for they are always perfect in our eyes. It's the behavior that needs re-adjustment now and then, not who they are. Be the parent. Have the tough conversations with them. Share yourself with all your foibles and mistakes that you made. They made you who you are, didn't they? Being the one to teach what boundaries are all about (saying NO!) really gives them the strength that they will need to travel through life and be the best that they CAN be.

My grandmother taught me another saying that has gotten me through a lot of rough times. It's called "*COUNT to 10*" and it was a gift from my grandmother. So follow along and see what you can glean from more of her wisdom.

Chapter 2

. . . .

The Hardest and Most Rewarding Job You'll Ever Have

Raising children is one of the hardest jobs today. But, it doesn't have to be. Come with me through a journey of helpful hints that can take some of the pressure off when parenting your child.

To begin with, my wise grandmother told me early on to Just *"Count to 10."* What she meant by that is that whenever I feel like I'm losing it with my children I must *"Count to 10"* before I engage in any action or communication. It helps you stop and instead of just re-acting to the situation you can assess the circumstance with reason and act accordingly.

Now that doesn't mean when your child is running out into the street you don't automatically grab them and save them. It means, be present when you communicate with your child. When our own stuff mixes in (having a bad day, the dryer broke, the dog's barking, you don't know where the money is going to come from to pay for the repair of that dryer). You now have a recipe for potential disaster.

To use the *"Count to 10"* method you simply do that in your head. And while you're counting, think:

- What is the real problem at hand?

- How dire is this situation?

- If I slow down my thoughts, can I get a better handle on this?

- What is really important here?

- Slow down, think, and take reasonable action and words.

"Counting to 10" can be as easy as 1-2-3. If you give yourself prompts that are meaningful to you, using the above only as an example, the *"Counting to 10"* can go quite quickly. The benefit you will gain is:

A calm communication with your child.

- Make use of a teaching moment.

- Being present in the moment.

- An outcome that you have orchestrated.

Communicating from a calm place will bring your voice level and tone down immediately. If you become hysterical, what happens? Right. They become either more hysterical themselves or at best continue in their behavior. You are the parent. You drive this bus. You are in charge and can make this situation the best that it can be along with teaching your child how to cope.

Afterwards, when they calm down too, you can ask them guided questions as to why the situation came up, what they need, how do they think they can best accomplish what they want and at the same time not anger someone else. When you use the "Count to 10" time to eliminate the dryer issue, money issue, and any other issues from your mind, you can now be present and take charge of the situation in the best way you can see possible. That's quite a different scenario, right? Not easy? Practice does make perfect.

Whenever we want to change something in ourselves we first must be aware of what it is we want to change. Then the next step is to believe you can do it. And finally, just do it!

I challenge you to take a situation and try *"Counting to 10"*.

- Clear your own mind of any extraneous thoughts.

- Become present to clearly think about the situation.

- Come up with a plan that can de-escalate the communication (soften your voice).

- Resolve what has come up with directness, understanding, and love.

- Try to maintain your sense of humor.

Parenting is a constant trial for you to be the best person you would like to model for your children. It's quite a daunting task if you take it down to each and every day. There are meditations you can use in the beginning of each day that simply state what your intention is for that day. Our thoughts drive our feelings, which drive our behavior, which gives us the results. Only you are in charge of your thoughts. But when we choose not to notice them and just go along with life chaos can and will show up.

For example: Jimmy and Ally are about four years old and arguing over who should have the crayon box. Ally hits Jimmy in order to get the crayon box from him. Jimmy let's go, but begins to cry and call, "Mommy!" You come around the corner having just spoken to the repair man about the dryer and found out it will be $95 just to see what's wrong with it.

In seeing Jimmy crying you would assume that Ally has done something to start this and you ask, "What's going on in here?!" in an irritated tone with a frown on your face, because of all that bad news you just got. "Why can't you two just play nicely with each other?" Jimmy explains loudly that Ally, "took the crayons from me and she hurt me!" You ask, "Ally, is that true? You know you shouldn't do that and it certainly is not okay to hit Jimmy. You know better." Continuing you make it <u>right</u>: "Ally, give the crayons back to Jimmy and share nicely." What do you think they have learned?

- If I cry loudly mommy will listen to me first. (Jimmy)

- I don't care if he cries I wanted the crayons. (Ally)

- She's so mad. I hate her. (Ally)

- She always sides with Jimmy. He's her favorite (Ally)

What if you *"Counted to 10"*? Put the anger away for now and deal with the situation. When I walk into the room I will ask both of the children what happened.

Now I have an opportunity to speak to them about how their actions have made the other one feel. We can brainstorm what would be a better way to get what each of them needs. "Let's sit down calmly and talk about what just happened. I was not in the room and I need you both to tell me what happened from your point of view."

Point out how Ally's action not only made Jimmy cry, but also become very unhappy because she took *all* of the crayons. Soothe Jimmy all the while by rubbing his back to help him calm down. Then, explaining that when we both want the same thing, problem-solve what would be a better way to get that so that the other person does not feel angry, hurt, or crying due to pain? "What would have been another way to do this, Ally? How about you, Jimmy? Do you have any ideas?" You can guide them through the answers and explanations.

You continue to go back and forth until they both see the benefit of a resolution and that physical force does not have to be the only way to get what you want. For instance, Ally could have asked Jimmy, "Jimmy I need some crayons too. Can we share?" Depending on their ages, you may have to give them the sentence stems to start out. That means giving them the beginning part of a sentence and letting them fill in the rest. Practicing this type of resolution in this way can bring not only peace but also understanding that our behavior affects everyone.

Now that that is finished, you can go back to your original thoughts of the dryer dilemma and probably are not as frustrated yourself. You can now think calmly and rationally and if not, count yourself a "10" to get to that reasonable thought process that you need as well.

We are so quick to anger, take actions without thinking first, and cause our own world of chaos at the same time. Can you see this? Doesn't it make sense to do some serious thinking about how we live each day? This is not rocket science; it is Universal Law showing up. We just have not "thought" of it in this way. ALL of our actions have consequences. When we become aware of how important the seemingly mundane things are, we need to do the work to change them.

No one said parenting was an easy job. No one warned us of how complicated these little darlings could be, or that we would have to use all our resources and constant "thinking" to get it done with some form of accomplishment. We don't get a degree once they are grown saying, "Passed with flying colors, Parent Judy." If you do take the time to *"Count to 10"* on a regular basis you can be guaranteed to accomplish more than you thought possible in "teaching" your children. The opportunities are endless.

Your patience in *"Counting to 10"* will pay off ten times over and in the process you yourself will be showing up as a positive role-model for your children. After all, isn't that what you are doing this for – to raise healthy, happy individuals?

Chapter 3

· ·

The Nuts and Bolts of "Counting to 10"

Now let's talk about the nuts and bolts of *"Counting to 10"*. You say, "I don't have enough time to *"Count to 10"* every five minutes." If the alternative is never positive, do you now have the time?

Time exists only in this plane of relativity. What happens if you do take the time to *"Count to 10"*? Stop and ask yourself some pertinent questions:

- What is the alternative of not taking the time?

- What outcome can I expect if I don't take the time?

- How does *"Counting to 10"* help me in this situation?

- What benefits are apparent to me when I do *"Count to 10"*?

- Are my children learning a better lesson from me when I *"Count to 10"*?

- How is my behavior affecting the situation when I *"Count to 10"*?

What does time really mean? Alice's adventure down the rabbit hole was a very concrete image when the poor rabbit could do nothing but run around frantically while his oversized alarm clock rang and stating, "I'm late, I'm late, for a very important date. No time to say Hello, Goodbye, I'm late, I'm late, I'm late!" How much do you suppose he got out of life as a rabbit? What would happen if we actually <u>did</u> take the time?

When we take the time to deliberately become present in our own lives, we are giving the gift of ourselves to all around us. Who shows up for you in your life when you bother to be aware of true time? The present has no past and has no future. It has been said that that is why it is called a "present." It has imminent power, gives valuable meaning to your life and thus awareness of what that life really is.

Wouldn't you choose to embrace your true power in your own life and realize (become aware) that YOU are the center of your children's universe for a very short time? The impact you can have on another human being is only limited to your own imagination. Why then do we take time so seriously? Why do we rush here and there to beat that proverbial clock and in the end, what has that done for us?

There is another way. Our awareness is all it takes to just "do it" differently. We can only change the things of which we are aware. In other words, THINK about it. Do you want to raise your children with true values? What are those values? Are you attending to them? Isn't it time to deliberately change for the better?

Here is a worksheet you can fill out together. Answer this simple question: What are the values we would like our children to grow up with and take with them in life? What qualities do you hope to help them develop?

Example: Honesty, respect for others, etc… Fill in here or use the "Workbook for Busy Moms".

Do you as parents think you can instill all these fabulous words into your children? It is a daily, awesome job. You can do it. We are all in this together, but your Job #1 listed below in the principles list is the key. "Inspiration," and guess who inspires us as children? Granted, it's not always your parents.

Sometimes it's a role model from outside your family. Whoever that person is or was for you, please take a moment and look at what you thought of them. What qualities did they model for you that you treasure? How do you want to change your parenting so you can become an excellent model for your children?

"Counting to 10" is only a metaphor for change. You are the vehicle of change and then only if YOU choose it. Let's set some guidelines down together that will ensure that we as parents can learn how to "do it" differently.

When you arise every morning what is your routine, Mom?

- Get up, brush my teeth

- Comb my hair & wash my face

- Put on my robe & slippers

- Pick up the baby & console any tears

- Change the diaper

- Heat up a bottle quickly

- Feed the baby & turn on the TV morning news

How could you do it differently? What would it look like if you spent just one minute on your intention for the day?

"Thank you, God, for this day. Today I intend to do my Best in every way. Please help me when I'm in need. I will see the goodness in all that I encounter and make the best of any situation for the betterment of my family and myself."

How long did that thought take? Not even a minute, but then again who's counting? Our thoughts are sooo important and we tend to not even realize them or pay attention to what goes on in our heads. What would your thought process be when you pick up your child, if you had started your day with your intention? Maybe something like this:

- Repeat the above intention before you get out of bed

- Say good-morning to myself with love while I'm brushing those teeth

- Smile as I hear the baby cry-asking for me-combing my hair, wash my face

- "I'm coming, Darling!" Put on my comfortable robe & slippers

- "Hush, Darling, Mommy is here. Good morning to you too! (Smile)

- "I wouldn't like this wet diaper either. Let's fix that!" (tickle tummy)

- Sing a familiar song while waiting for the bottle

- "Oh, how I love this time with you. Let's cuddle & drink together. I have my coffee & you have your bah."

- Hum that simple song quietly while you smooth that unruly hair

Can you do this? Of course, there are times when we just had a bad night, no sleep in so long, cold in the winter, hot in the summer. But it is ALWAYS our choice as to how we perceive a situation and then choose how to be in it. That's being "present."

Did you need to *Count to 10* this morning? Did it make you more present? What were the thoughts running through your head? *Counting to 10* simply gives you the focus to think about what you want to attend to in your thoughts. It can make it possible for you to be actually present in the moment which only means being aware of yourself in the circumstance.

Chapter 4

. . . .

Rules to Live By

When beginning to learn parenting and *"Counting to 10"* there are some prerequisites I'd like to share with you.

"Counting to 10" helps you *think* first and avoid worrying about saying "no" to everything – while at the same time hating to say it.

Every house needs "Rules to Live By" and they must be communicated at an early age, changed as the child grows, and even turning into "contracts" as they become teenagers.

What are your "Rules" for the house? Write them down, post them (refrigerators are well known for this use) and follow them. That means, YOU – the parents must follow the "Rules." Your job once you have written them is to: 1) communicate them with explanation 2) get on board with each other in agreeing that both parents are to implement them, and how 3) design and agree on consequences, if they are not followed and 4) be consistent, consistent, consistent.

We don't often put "Rules" in the proper context. For young children when you are explaining what rules are, you need to convey that: "In our house these are the rules." When they get older and go off to other peoples houses to play and they find out not everyone has the same rules, you must remember to explain this. "I know Johnny doesn't have the same rules at his house. So when you are there you follow Mrs. Aldon's rules. But, our family rules do apply there too. What I mean by that is that wherever you go, our house rules apply as well."

You are teaching them early on that what we do when no one else is looking (or keeping "rules" like my house) is right. It begins that inner locus of control that will be very important throughout their lives.

When a child learns to trust his family's rules and values, it is something that will be ingrained in him and guide him to his own inner voice that will be telling him what is right and wrong, no matter what his friends say or do. It is a powerful tool you will be giving him and one that is not always talked about until as adults they realize they have it.

You may never hear it, but their actions will show you through time. If we *think* ahead, "rules" are nothing more than the prerequisite to "Laws." That big world out there that does have such things like "Do Not Drink and Drive," or "21 Is The Legal Drinking Age." *Think* about it.

You have actually just done an exercise in learning the Law of Attraction. First you have to identify what it is you want. You wrote down the rules. Then you have to believe that you can. Practice until it works. And last, but not least, take action with commitment and consistency. So here I will give you an example of your possible "Rules" list:

OUR HOUSE RULES

No hitting, biting, or whining

Listen to Mommy and Daddy

Eat at the Table

Bed Time is: _____

Ask Permission for Snacks

Come Get Me If You Need My Help

The first line is self-explanatory. You need to know that if these behaviors are occurring in your house the responsibility to understand them and change the behavior starts with you. Any child who is screaming, hitting, biting, or whining is asking for your attention. Are you giving them what they NEED?

All children basically need to believe that they are lovable and acceptable. Their lovability quotient comes from how you respect their wants and needs in how you interact with them. Of course, we all lose it at times, but your inner voice should be saying to you "What message am I conveying?"

For example, if you put yourself in your child's shoes and come into a room and see a person with a frown on their face, what do you think? That they are angry with you, are going to yell at you, hurt you, or make you feel bad.

When you *THINK* first as if you are the child, how does it look now? "*Counting to 10*" will teach you how to think from a different perspective. Young children cannot say to you, "Mommy, I'm feeling disrespected because Jimmy took my toy and I'm really angry so I have to take my frustration out by hitting him." Go that extra mile to understand where your child is coming from and help them to find the words they need to tell you how they feel.

How do you do this? You simply ask questions of them that speak about their feelings. Feelings will give you an insight into their thoughts, where you can make a difference in how they *think*. Children can be taught this as young as two years old. If you've ever learned a second language, you know that you can understand much more than you can speak at first, right? This is true of children learning their first language.

They "get" body movement and posturing as well. They "get" feeling loved, adored, accepted, and cared for. They "get" feeling hated, or being the cause of someone's anger, and end up carrying thoughts of being unacceptable, loathed, unimportant, shamed, or guilty. How much longer is the latter list?

Our own personal issues come into play when a child's behavior annoys us, or angers us, and over-reaction happens. "*Counting to 10*" could save you a lot of anguish from repeated behavior that you as the parent have taught your child.

Learned behavior is often times developed from re-action to our parents. If you take apart that word (re-action), look at it again. Re denotes "again" and action is the behavior. We teach our children trigger points. Those trigger points last a lifetime, don't they? Do you know why that angry look on your husband's face set you off today over such a silly little thing? That was your learned behavior, your trigger point. If your child sets one off in you without "*Counting to 10*" and getting a grip on reality (not your trigger point) you will be laying the same groundwork for them.

We can't become perfect parents because there are none. We all do the best we can with what we have at the time. If just *thinking* could make that much of a change wouldn't you want to? What can we lose if we don't try? Evidently a lot.

I know you've heard many times that a temper tantrum is best ignored. Let's look at what happens to make a neuropathway that ingrains this behavior.

What happens when Johnny starts to scream as you say No! to a treat just before dinner? The first time you pick him up and explain, "Johnny, you can have a treat after dinner." Does that stop the behavior? Of course not.

What have you just done? You picked him up and gave him attention. He doesn't care how he got it. Just that he did. Now keep going for a couple of weeks and see if the unwanted screaming behavior lessens. It doesn't, does it? How else could you do this? Let's THINK.

Get down on Johnny's level, eye-ball-to-eye-ball and looking straight in. "Johnny, screaming is not acceptable in our house. You know the rules. It's almost dinnertime so let's get ready by washing our hands. We are having chicken tonight, your favorite!"

Changing the subject always helps, but I know I did a lot of <u>this</u> – at the end of that sentence do you say, "okay?" You really don't want to have an answer, do you? To stay in the affirmative, train yourself not to ask this question. You will become very adept at stating what behavior you want and much more likely to get it.

Ask for what you want. That little toddler who understands so much is always striving to please you. Ask what the behavior is that you want. Speak directly and with a smile on your face.

Here's a great thought to keep in mind. If you want your children to feel love on a regular basis "just smile." Every time they walk into a room (at any age) "just smile" and show that you are truly happier to see their face. Your eyes and expression say it all.

This is all about learning HOW to *think*. It's amazing the changes we can make when we realize the only one capable of changing anything is ourselves. If I *"Count to10"* and use my thoughts to show my feelings of authority with caring, I can create the behavior I'm looking for and get the results we all want! It's a win-win!

Now practice by taking a few minutes here and "pick apart" your own most recent scenario. Rebuild it using the *"Count to 10"* method and remember to start with your thoughts, that generate your feelings, that create your behavior, that accomplishes the result. If you can't get this, or need some help Just Call Your Coach!

Go to <u>www.helpformomcoach.com</u> to make an appointment with Sue.

Don't forget that we are making *new* neuropathways in your brain. We are using repetition to <u>replace</u> old neuropathways that are like ruts formed in our brain from past thoughts, feelings, and old stories. This does take patience and commitment. Change comes only from awareness. So don't give up too easily. Practice, practice, practice and start small. Even try a positive behavior that you already see in your child. Look at how you engage and act with them at those times. Their neuropathways are forming now too.

Now do the "pick apart" exercise here. Take your scenario and think backwards to the beginning and see what you can discover. That is, what was the outcome (result)of you and your child's behavior? How were you feeling before that? What thoughts did you have and imagine what your child's thoughts were too? Read on for more information about the Model of Human Functioning.

Chapter 5

. . . .

The Model of Human Functioning

There is a Model of Human Functioning that explains very well the process we go through that gives us the results of our behavior. The question is whether we are living from the **Outside-In** or the **Inside-Out**. In other words, do you live your life by circumstance and allow your world outside to be the only influence on your behavior? Or can you relate to living your life from the **Inside-Out**? The obvious notion that you let your world on the outside drive your thoughts is a reactive one. You only observe what you see and react to it.

Your true power over how your life goes comes from the inside. If you live by paying attention to your thoughts first, you get a very different scenario. Our thoughts influence our feelings that give us the behavior, which results in_____. You fill in the blank. Thoughts are much more important than you may think. Pay attention to your thoughts because "what you attend to expands."

This is a Universal Law. You are the driver of this ride called life. God gave us free will, which is the choices that we make, but if you're not paying attention to the thoughts, who's driving?

Here is an explanation and example: When we choose to attend to our thoughts, we can understand the magnitude of them. Here's the question: Which way are you living? From the **Inside-Out** or from the **Outside-In**?

LIVING FROM THE OUTSIDE-IN or FROM THE INSIDE-OUT
YOUR CHOICE:

	RESULTS	
OUTSIDE ----→	**BEHAVIOR**	**←---- INSIDE**
	FEELINGS	
	THOUGHTS	

Living from the **Outside-In** means that we <u>react</u> to life (not always the result we want). Living from the **Inside-Out** allows us to change our results by being <u>aware</u> of our thoughts. Remember, you cannot change anything if you are not aware of it.

We are working from the bottom to the top in this diagram. Since our thoughts cause the feelings we have, which drives our behavior, that gives us the result – look how attending to our thoughts magnifies into the result.

To be cognizant of our thoughts (by slowing down the mind as in *"Counting to 10"*) it will allow you to choose how the feelings will be, thus the behavior (action), thus the result can be positive, even in a negative situation.

EXAMPLE SITUATION: Living from the Outside-In. Johnny comes home from high school saying, "I'm not going to graduate!! My counselor told me that I have too many absences without doctor's notes. How am I going to go to college? My life is ruined!" Normally, for Mom, the thought would rush right out of her mouth, "Oh, no! What will we do? You know, that counselor should have told you sooner. She's responsible for your well being and she knows you are accepted at college already. What is she thinking?" This would elevate the conversation into the extreme with yelling something like this, "Why didn't you…" You know the story.

Living from the **Inside-Out** the scenario could be: Johnny says, "I'm *not* going to graduate!! I have too many absences without doctor's notes. My counselor told me! How am I going to go to college? My life is ruined!" When mom *"Counts to 10"* before responding and pays attention to her thoughts by living from the **Inside-Out** she could say, "Well, Johnny, let's see what you can do to change that. What ideas can you come up with?"

Mom has not only thought to look at this from a positive angle she has given that gift to her son. Also after de-escalating the drama, she put the ownership on Johnny (where it belongs) to come up with a solution.

In using the "what" question to her son Mom has moved a potentially volatile situation (reactive) to encouragement and a pro-active thinking process by her son.

Can you see that the awareness of thought, which is a simple, conscious thinking, naturally changes (*"Count to 10"*) REACTION into PRO-ACTIVE behavior and the result is positive? Pretty amazing, right?

Take a sheet of paper and write down a situation that has occurred in your life with the perspective coming from the Result backwards to the Thought. Then take another sheet of paper and write the same situation from the Thought – after *"Counting to 10"*, all the way up to the Result and see what comes up for you.

Chapter 6

· ·

The Mad Hatter's Tea Party

"Counting to 10" is a trick for our brains to slow down, listen to our thoughts and if they are not what we want, change them. The merry-go-round of life today tells us that we are all the "Rabbit" and time is getting away from us. We'd better hurry. But where are we hurrying to? Let's *think* differently. Let's use time as a friend. It takes just as much time to have a negative thought as it does to have a positive one. But you can have only one thought at a time. Which kind do you want? This is not a new idea.

That peanut butter and jelly sandwich smudged all over Jeffrey's face (he is just learning how to get food from the plate to the mouth!) is not dire. Kids are messy, Mom. Lighten up and laugh a bit. Get the washcloth after he's all done making a mess. That sandwich certainly tasted much better, didn't it? He thinks so. He's thinking: "Mommy wasn't yelling at me because I was too messy. In fact, she laughed at how funny I looked!"

That was your choice to see it funny instead of dire. All day you can make these same choices for yourself and realize you're making that choice for them too. They will see you in the light that you intend. Which is better, a frazzled, up-tight, yelling Mom or a loving, laughing, appreciative Mom? Your choice. Your thoughts.

Law of Attraction: What you focus on expands. If our thoughts run in the negative vein we will produce negative behavior, negative habits, thus a negative life. Using *"Count to 10"* can help you to take the time to be aware of what you are focusing on. You will get more of whatever that is. Can you now see that each thought is sooo important? Too much to handle? Maybe. So just call your Coach. Go to www.helpformomcoach.com . This life is meant to be FUN! Let's work together to make it so. Together we can find your bliss so you can pass that on to your children.

Don't let your "life" get any more daunting. Having a coach can make everything you've been reading about happen for you. Release your fears and move to a better place when you attend to your thoughts. Can you do this? Of course, you can. If you need some help just ask. Where are you right now? In the "present" perhaps? "Now is as good a time as any." It's a platitude, but it's true.

We as a human race have a lot of work to do in figuring out how to live this life. Parents are the ones who will be molding the future of our children. What we inculcate in them is our legacy to them. How amazing is that? Are you ready to *"Count to 10"* yet? Do you have the TIME?

This job of learning how to parent is tough. I've been there, but I do know it doesn't have to be that hard. Coaching is not about "telling" you what to do. It's all about you discovering what you want in life with a guide who helps you to accomplish those dreams. There is someone there for you without judgment who keeps you centered and accountable to enable you to grow far beyond what you even thought you could do. You don't have to go it alone.

We have to BE the grown up when we have children. We are in charge of their well being, their safety, and their growth. How we got off the track of guiding them lovingly and having to be a friend instead was a big wrong turn. Our children love us more unconditionally than we realize.

Our children may be angry at us once in a while, but they do not remove love because of it. Don't you love your children even when you are angry at them? You aren't angry at "them," your are disappointed in their behavior. Love is always there. It's both our safety nets. Family first. Are you living like the Rabbit?

Respect comes from giving it. Love comes from giving it. Forgiveness comes from giving it. Allow your children to fall and learn from their own consequences. Your job is to be there for them (that safety net) *if* they ask for advice when they're grown. Just being their parent with a firm grasp on life (you do have wisdom from your own experiences in life) is your gift for them. If you're there for them in this gentle, knowing, loving way, trust me they are there for you as well. Communication, communication, communication.

Chapter 7

· ·

Does Your Teenager Look Like An Adult?

"Counting to 10" does not have to stop when your children become teenagers. Can you think of a better time to give yourself a pass on negativity and try to turn the situation around? When we realize that our children are simply in a larger body and they really aren't equipped to be the adults that we assume they are, just because of their size, take a breath. Whew! You mean my sixteen-year-old is not as responsible, clear headed, and all knowing as he claims to be? Ha!

Now at least there's a chance to change some things. We all still have time as parents to have an influence. Are you happier yet? Have you figured out what they are up to and where exactly you fit in? Let's re-visit the rules from the toddler stages.

- Who sets the limits?

- Who is in charge?

- How much do you listen?

- Who sets the parameters?

- How long a rein do you give them before you pull it in?

- Am I focusing on what's important here?

- What do I need to be aware of that needs change?

Parents are now more than ever the stabilizing influence on their children. You do think it's the outside world that they have joined (friends, teachers, significant relationships) that has all the power, influence, and importance. Don't give up the ship yet! YOU, the parents are not playing dead, are you? Or is it just that you don't know what to do? You can Just Call Your Coach. Try this: *"Count to 10"* and ask yourself the relevant questions above. What are your answers?

By this point in the child's life we get tired. We worked so hard in those formative years with each and every stage being of utmost importance. Who gave you permission to give up now just because they are telling you that you are insignificant to them?

If you have done all your homework, you would know that teenagers need to experiment with all different personas. They need to take risks and fail in many different ways before they learn the lessons. Sadly, we as parents take the responsibility away from them by telling them what to do, setting limits that seem to change as a moving target, and try to conform them into something or someone they don't want to be. We are the ones who are going to get the consequences. They may come to us through our children, but we don't even see it as such.

I have a friend who was concerned about her son, Joey, because he seemed to be unmotivated both at school and at home. She couldn't figure out why this bright, well-mannered, quiet, young man was turning inward. After all, the two girls she raised before him were out in the world, college, with friends and good grades. What was so different for Joey?

The one thing that was different was that his sisters were expected to clean their own rooms, do laundry and help out in the kitchen. But since Joey is the youngest he was spared such chores. After all, he was the only boy, the last one home and Mom felt sorry for him. She felt bad that he didn't have his sisters to jolly up the house. It was quiet now and he was, after all, stuck with Mom & Dad. Mom had the time to do everything for him as she always had.

We talked about responsibility. I asked her, what chores does Joey have now? It was "simpler" for her to do them. What else would she be doing? Can you see where this is going? Sometimes when we are in the moment, we just don't think.

It was easier for Mom to do it all. She would have to change if she quit some of the chores because Joey was doing them. But in reality Joey was getting bored when home. Not having many friends in his new school was not helping. Not doing well in school was bringing the wrath of Dad down on him. No responsibility at home only added to his feelings of worthlessness.

Mom was in need of changing her life by giving up some of her own "jobs" that might fill up some of Joey's time and also give him a feeling of accomplishment, a job well done, and contributing to the family.

Remember the principles and values you wanted to impart to your children when you started out on this road of life? Have you forgotten them? Do you still talk about them? Encourage it in your child? Probably not. Life gets in the way. TIME is too important, "I'm late, I'm late, I'm late…"

Some things that fell by the wayside for Joey's family:

- Weekly Family Meetings

- Chores to be completed as charted on the fridge

- Family Mandatory Fun

- Late night talks

- Tucking in at night

- Anyone home when Joey leaves, anyone home when he returns

We don't intentionally forego the structure in our daily lives. It just seems to happen to us without our knowing. When our family structure changes radically as when siblings move on, we don't pay attention. What happens to what we focus on seems to be what life is meant to be. Changes just happened while we were busy doing life. Take heart. The things that we notice and are aware of, can still be changed.

Life is really one big change after another. So what is so different now? I think we are tired from our jobs, from everyday situations we all go through in life. Your job is not done, so haul yourself up, take a good look, focus, and change again. One more time. That one more time will continue until we pass to another realm. Getting tired comes from NOT stopping, thinking, paying attention to those thoughts, realizing that we created where we are NOW.

Basically, what I'm saying here is that if it isn't working for you now, CHANGE IT! Have a meeting of the minds with each other as parents. Re-group and center on what you want to be different. It's all up to you, parents.

Here is another place in time where you want to focus on the positive so you don't lose your mind. Teenagers are trying, there's no getting around it. But here is where your practice of gratitude focusing can also help.

Moms hate to say No. It seems easier at this age when actually they are just testing your limits again. Do you STILL hate to say No? Have you learned better ways to express yourself in words? Are you worried that Johnny will not love you if you say No! one more time?

This is a test. The real question is: Do you so desperately want to be their "friend" that you will say yes to almost anything, even when you know you shouldn't? I'm going to tell you a secret: You are their parents, and they love you anyway. They may get angry with you or even say, "I hate you!" Don't take it personally. You will survive their anger.

Stick to your beliefs and values and they will come around. You do not have to even argue with them about it. Just state your case, and what it is you expect of them. Let them know that you believe in them enough to know that they will make the right choice, and walk away.

Now when they don't make the right choice you can also prove that love by standing by their side in problem solving, BUT, only if they ask. Their struggles are just like yours. Mistakes are only that, mistakes. They are still loved.

Next time they have a chance to make a <u>better</u> choice and you are still there for them. Cheer on their growth in what they learn through mistakes. You did it. They can too.

Something that was true for us in our family was an eye opener when it happened to me. My husband was being particularly critical of one child and inappropriately berating. In speaking to him about it afterwards I asked, "Why did you handle it that way?" He simply explained, "Well, I don't know what else to do. I can't think of another way to get him to do what I want – the right thing."

Remember to Just Call Your Coach. Go to: www.helpformomcoach.com. There are always answers to any dilemma. It's a good thing to admit that sometimes we just don't know HOW to deal with our children. We haven't dealt with the same circumstances in our past so we don't seem to have a map.

I remember a saying that just sticks in my head, "The dumbest question is always the one that isn't asked."

Work with a coach to resolve conflict, find answers that may just tweak your imagination to do it differently in your family. Being open to change is simply being aware that it is needed. Good for you.

Chapter 8

· ·

Practice, Practice, Practice

"Counting to 10" is all-important at any stage your child may be in. If you think it went well once you got the hang of it when they were toddlers then here is another challenge: Teenagers. Here's how it works in this venue:

Patience is a virtue. Who said that? It also comes with practice, practice, practice and more practice. Our children can try our patience more than any friend, parent, sibling, or anyone else you can think of. They have a knack of setting us off the mark with a bang. It's just like real estate's mantra of location, location, location. You might not like the time it takes to learn patience, but in the end you will be the one to benefit from it first.

Detaching occurs with *"Counting to 10"* as well and in this period of your child's life is absolutely a necessity. It does not mean to stop caring, but to not be invested in the outcome. Stepping back and being present in the moment will give you the wisdom that you need. Remember to share these insights with your spouse and discuss your common ground.

When you as parents have come to the playing field with consistency, and united, unflagging commitment, you are a formidable force to be reckoned with. Do not discount this statement. It could be the biggest tool in your toolbox of coping skills. When you have mastered this one you are well on your way of avoiding a lot of heartache and disappointment in yourself as well as your teen.

Once you have a plan in hand with regard to how you both have committed to each other to deal sanely with your teenager you are ahead of the game already.

Planning is of utmost importance and here is a guideline you can alter to fit your principles for your family.

What are the family principles that you want to reiterate now?

The Hyde School in Woodstock, Connecticut has a very good idea that you could take and use for your family. They are a character based learning high school with several campuses in the eastern United States. The definition for principle is: integrity, rule of conduct.

PRINCIPLES TO LIVE BY:

Truth over harmony. In our house it took my youngest going to The Hyde School to teach us as parents true values. To live your life with this as a guide takes guts. To be a parent and to do this with your children watching is truly learning humility. When we step over difficult situations to keep the peace in the household we are living by harmony, not truth.

If say your teenager comes in with an "attitude" that is not respectful what do you usually do? Step over it; tell ourselves, "That's a teenager for you. He must be having a bad day." We are then living in harmony - meaning <u>anything</u> for peace in this moment, but is that true? We as parents often find it is "easier" to avoid talking about the truth. He has a bad attitude, is being disrespectful.

What is the truth? What are our options in this present moment? We could always step over it, as mentioned, or we could have a discussion with him and discern what "his" problem might be. Talking to a non-communicative teen is a challenge, but if we never step over any situation we would have a bigger chance to communicate.

However the conversation goes it is not a license to drive home your "disrespectful *lecture*." True compassion for what is true for your child opens doors to how they are.

You have an opportunity to know who they really are and what is going on for them by keeping communication open. If it's just a bad mood, we all have them, but what is the cause underneath that? If your family principle is to respect all who enter in, say so.

Principles over rules. When we use the word "rules" it often times sets people off, especially young adults. It seemed to work when we had charts on the refrigerator when they were young, but suddenly it is a bone of contention. Discuss at Family Meetings what your principles are. Make sure everyone understands them from a very young age, or start NOW and then refer to them as "principles" when the correct time comes. A "rule" by most teenagers' standards is the thing that needs to be broken. Principles are what we live by to show our integrity.

Attitude over aptitude. When your children's attitude is <u>more</u> <u>important</u> than what they produce, for example grades from school, you're on the right track. We cannot all be math wizards, or history buffs. What is your child's strength? That is what is to be encouraged, no matter what the grades. *Are they doing their BEST?*

The attitude comes in when you look at how they are performing. Have they given it their all? Is there a best-shot notable to you? Ask them, "Have you given this your 100% best?" If not, what is standing in your way? How can I help you?

You can even relate this to a teenager in regard to their aptitude with attitude. Can they or do they have the capacity (aptitude) to respect those living with them? Then here is your chance to explain that that is what is expected of them.

Set high expectations and let go of the outcome. When our children have a very clear picture of what is expected of them it is their responsibility to produce that. If your child who was so accommodating and tried sooo hard to gain your approval at a young age suddenly could care less, hang on!

Hold true to your principles but let the consequence of their behavior belong to them (let go of the outcome). How often do we "help" with schoolwork to the point of the ridiculous? Whose job is it anyway?

They cannot learn unless they are allowed to make the mistakes themselves. It is NOT, I repeat NOT a reflection on you if they are getting bad grades, not finishing homework, dressing like a slob (your opinion). Your job is to do what? Not DO the work for them but find out what is making this underline expectation of them so low.

Having a heart-to-heart often with your teen will reiterate the family principles while also letting them know you are still there. When we do for them the message is, "I know you can't do it to my standards, so I'll do it for you." That is your hidden message when you "help" with school work, or any other thing you do instead of allowing them.

Often times we praise thinking that is going to build good self-esteem. My daughter stopped me short on that one once. "Sweetheart, I know you can do it – you always do such a good job." She shared with me, "But that's not true, Mom. I know everyone always says that I can but the truth is – I can't and I don't know why!" Who's helping whose self-esteem???

Sometimes when your teen shows no apparent "listening" skills going on you simply state your concern, show support emotionally and move on (underline leave the room). Don't wait for an answer and when it is not forthcoming, keep talking. You will have committed the ultimate sin as written by a teenager, "They keep saying the same thing over and over again. I'm so sick of it!" Trust me, they heard you the first time.

Value success AND failure. Some of the biggest teaching moments in life come from our failures, right? When we do not let our children fail, what have they learned? Usually nothing. They may even be saying to themselves: "Mom or Dad usually picks up the slack. If I tell Mom my project is due tomorrow I know she'll pull out all the stops, go to the stationery store for the markers and poster board that I need and do most of the work." If you don't do this the misery they will feel the next day in class when they have nothing (or possibly a slapped together project) is worth everything.

Who do you think will work harder not to have that humiliating feeling in class again? Now if you have someone with time-management problems you probably have been working on this since 2nd grade.

Successes can be valued when they are not an A too! What you know your child is capable of is a success when they have put in their best. Valuing them as a person is always important, but the struggles are where the gems of life lie. Talk about the lesson in the failure. Oops! I mean ask them what they have learned from the situation.

Do not speak for them; let the silence carry their thoughts. There is no underlining necessary when silence brings up their truth. Encourage them to share by being silent, just holding the space for them. Trust me, they'll get it.

Allow obstacles to become opportunities. When we see our children struggling with peer pressure, difficulties in school, or hard times of any kind we tend to jump right in and save them. Instead, as a parent who is more aware, you can speak to them about the gems that are found in the struggles. Teaching by example is always good because a "story" makes it interesting and meaningful. So tell some of your stories to your children about the struggles you've had and the connection will be appreciated.

You know how we try to be the "Joneses"? Everything is always just FINE. In admitting to our truths we set our families free from having to pretend. It enables us to see the challenges we face as striving to be our best. It will enable growth to spring forth and ease the dependence of "perfection" as a measurement of success. Open up discussions of these difficult subjects and you will find ingenious ways to look at obstacles; many of which will come from your children.

Take hold and let go. This is one of my favorite subjects because it always brings back a memory from a Hyde weekend (the character-based high school in Connecticut my daughter attended). One particular seminar weekend, we had an interesting task to complete.

As an object of learning, this concept of hanging on and letting go we learned while attending Hyde. Let me explain. The whole exercise was physically doing what we needed to learn ourselves. The task was that we had to climb up a ladder beside a tree and then climb up three wooden posts on the tree. All this to get to a rope strung taughtly between this and another tree.

Then we had to walk sideways (inch your way) across with only a perpendicular rope to grasp that dangled above your head. There were three of these ropes set apart every eight feet. In order to grab hold of the second dangling rope, one had to let go of the first.

We had on helmets, climbing gear, and our spouse or partner to belay you from the ground below (in case you "fell"). I made it to the second dangling rope only after falling onto the rope I was standing on. With the help of my husband pulling me up too (that's the belay part. Talk about trust?). I somehow pulled myself back up totally by my arms to get to continue. It was physically one of the hardest things I have ever had to do, but truly gratifying in that I didn't give up!

This exercise was done to understand how hard it is at times to take hold of our children as a concerned parent (as we were in deciding to send her away to Hyde) and then let go because *she* was in charge of her destiny. *She* was the one that had to do her own work (while we were doing ours).

It is a very hard lesson, but if you can take hold of what you have taught your family in values and principles, you must also let go and trust that they are in there. Their journey is theirs, not ours.

Our children will learn by our example of *living our lives* with the same principles. When we focus totally on them we give up our journey, that's how living vicariously through our children happens.

Chapter 9

. . . .

Teach How To "Be" Your Best, It's Better Than A's!

It took me a long time to put this little book together. I have collected just some of the reflections on raising my children. They have been my greatest teachers in many ways.

What I'm hoping is that when you finish reading this you will feel much better equipped to carry on your own journey as parents and add your own bits of wisdom.

We need to be more vulnerable with each other in order to share the hard times as well as the good. If we start by teaching our children awareness and actually live by it too, just think what a better world they can have by their own contributions.

Our children are our gifts. They are *often* our biggest teachers. They are certainly our most precious hope for the future. Let us all come together and raise humanity to what it could be. Think BIG. Encourage your children to BE their best, as well as ourselves. In so doing you can say in the end, "Job Well Done!" Give *yourself* the Star. Please notice I didn't say *perfect* job!

This title we call "MOM" (and don't forget "DAD") will fill your heart to overflowing and give back to each and every one of us, ten fold.

Let LOVE be your guide,

God Bless

Now please continue on and use the workbook to further expand your thought process for some conscious parenting.

Chapter 10

. . . .

Workbook for Busy Moms

Reminder: *What You Attend to or Focus On Expands*

This is a simple guideline book on changing what you want to change in your every-day life. Set up your own steps to improve yourself and how you want to be as a parent. **Reminders** are topics to *think* about as your day unfolds. Enjoy!

What is my intention for this day? I plan on giving only love to those around me and staying centered knowing that I am the most important person in this "little person's" life.

To begin my day positively I will listen to the cry of my baby and know that he is talking to me to help him. Is it a cry for food? Does my little one hate to be wet and uncomfortable? How shall we dress today? Cold? Hot?

Comfort comes with holding, cuddling, speaking softly, and smiling as you meet each other's eyes in the morning. The crying may not stop immediately, but I know that he/she is depending upon me for everything in his/her little world.

At the end of the day (seven days listed) take a moment to write:

Today I learned _____

_____

_____

_____

_____

_____ about my child.

Today I learned _____

_____

_____

_____

_____

_____

_____ about my child.

Today I learned _____

_____

_____

_____

_____

_____

_____ about my child.

Today I learned _____

_____

_____

_____

_____

_____

_____ about my child.

Today I learned _____

_____

_____

_____

_____

_____ about my child.

Today I learned _____

_____

_____

_____

_____ about my child.

Today I learned _____

_____

_____

_____

_____ about my child.

Reminder: *THINK About What and How You Believe Child Raising Will Impact Your Children*

Write that down here.

What I learned about myself:

_____

_____

_____

_____

_____

Pick up a notebook to continue this exercise and do it on a daily/weekly basis and share it with your partner. Have some fun with it and laugh about the stories that will come up from your childhood. Get to know each other on a deeper level and you'll be surprised how understanding we can be with one another. Understanding always comes before acceptance. In accepting one another's reality in childhood we can grow into responsible parents and not just react from our past.

If you take apart words it is interesting what you can find. For example, that word "react". Re-act now says to us: to act in the same way as before. A repeat action is one that comes without thinking. Isn't that what a "trigger" is, in the context of relationships? Well, when we haven't taken out the "triggers" that happen when parenting and really understand them we will create the same experience for our children. *Think* about it. In order to grow up our past, that is, to bring the past into the present (but with adult understanding), it takes awareness.

We can help one another to do this by talking about it, understanding it (from both viewpoints) and, by becoming aware that we now choose to do this differently. Learning to listen consciously to each other can be done when you repeat back to the person what you heard them say. You not only become a better listener through this exercise, but you think more about what you are intending. How clear are you in communicating?

Reminder: *What About Your Childhood?*

Now ask yourself some questions. How did I cope with my own *feelings* about my childhood? Do I know where my triggers come from? How can I do this a better way?

Emotional Freedom Technique (EFT) is a technique that you can easily learn that will get you in touch with your inner self and work on feelings that need healing in order for you to be the Best that you can be. We all have "trigger points" that go back to our childhoods, but let's stop making them hinder our relationships, especially with our children. Go to: www.emofree.com to learn more about this technique for free. How we interact with our children is important from the very beginning. We spend a huge amount of time before the birth on knowing what happens at each stage of development. We take La Maize classes to prepare us for the delivery. But the real work comes when they arrive.

We take our dogs to training school and find that we are really training ourselves. We go to driving school to get our license to drive a car. We've spent how many *years* educating ourselves to be able to perform to our best in the profession we choose called "work." So how much time have you spent on readying yourselves for the most important job you'll ever have, parenting?

This topic is not meant to make you feel bad. It's to wake us all up and realize that our most precious commodity in life (our children) takes a lifetime to learn. Want some help? This workbook is to make you *think* about what and how you believe child raising will impact your children. Dig deep and answer all of the questions herein honestly and completely. You can journal every day and discover for yourself where your hurdles, questions, challenges lie. Simply ask a question at the top of the page and write about that subject. Keep writing until you have no more to say about it. You'll be amazed at what you learn. Go ahead and practice here until you get the hang of it...

My question is: _____

_____

_____

_____

_____

_____

Reminder: *What Are Your Goals?*

_____

_____

_____

_____

_____

_____

_____

_____

_____

_____

_____

_____

NOW that you are aware of the above discoveries, you can make changes to truly create what you want for your family. Do this together. Parents include "Dad" too after all. To start your own "plan" we need to set some goals for your family (long-term and short-term).

Take the time to discuss this with each other. Decide how you want to work as a team in raising your children. Togetherness was never so important as it is in parenting. From this moment on, a secret ingredient to great parenting is to be on the same page. Co-parenting is what it should be called. Presenting a united front will benefit your whole family over and over again. So since you have done the past exercises to see what needs tweaking in your own personal family guide let's keep going.

Short-term goals means what you want to accomplish this week, etc. Take some notes on what you both want from parenting. How do you see your child's development in two years, four years, etc.? Plan this out because without a map or plan, how will you get there?

It's true. A map helps us navigate to where we want to go, right? Plans are the same tool but in this context it is for what you want to accomplish in your lives together. It is imperative to have short-term and long-term goals for your family. The road maps that you create now will be an integral part in your parenting. What is your plan? To prepare you for the next exercise *think* about this for a moment. Was your parent's style of bringing you up "authoritative" or "permissive?" In an authoritative home it is more like a dictatorship. Ruled from above and no questions asked – just do what you're told and everything will be "fine." Or perhaps you came from a permissive atmosphere where whatever comes just "go with the flow." Bed time in a permissive household is: whenever they get tired.

Reminder: *Set Out Your Own Plan.*

These topics were not brought up when you were in the first stage of "love" so fasten your seat belt now. It's like, "What type of X-Mas tree should we get for our first holiday?" Did that question cause chaos?

Discuss the specific ways you were both brought up and write them down here:

Mom: _____

_____

_____

_____

_____

_____

_____

_____

Dad:_____

_____

_____

_____

_____

_____

_____

_____

_____

Reminder: *Parenting Skills We Agree On.*

Now write down what sort of parenting skills you **agree** upon. Be specific about the things you **disagree** on, **compromise** and make it an agreement instead. Just because that was the way it was for us individually, in the past, does not mean that it has to be that way now. The more you are willing to change your mind (awareness that consciously you can make it your own together) the better chance you have of being the leaders in your child's life.

By modeling for your children what compromise is at the earliest age will teach them how to do it. You will be revisiting this page again and again as they grow. Just because they aren't "old enough" to understand doesn't mean they don't benefit from you with your actions. Take some time and write them down here:

Parenting skills we agree on: _____

_____

_____

_____

_____

_____

_____

_____

_____

You do not have to raise your children as you were raised. We will do it the same way unless we intentionally look at our past upbringing, agree or disagree with it, and make the appropriate changes that we both agree upon.

There will be times that we individually fall back into old patterns, or new ones come up that we didn't discuss before. It's okay! Simply talk about it calmly and agree again. Communication, remember? Just do it again.

To be aware of our old habits is the beginning. The awareness that comes from recognizing it allows us to re-write the dialogue together: CHANGE IT. A good tip on knowing when we are triggered is to ask the question: "Am I over-reacting to this situation?" Bingo! Just be aware, and now you can consciously accept what was and begin again. Your intention now can be clear.

Below, start your short-term goals by being very specific on how you are to BE with your child. Take all the information you have collected from each other and write down what parenting is to you together.

Reminder: *Short-term Goals to Agree On.*

Create your own short-term goals: _____

_____

_____

_____

_____

_____

_____

Create your own long-term goals: _____

_____

_____

_____

_____

_____

_____

Feel good about this exercise? Just remember that you can revamp, revisit, re-write anything on these pages. The trick is to *agree* upon what you change.

The next part of the workbook is going to be more specific in that we will delve into more of the "how to's" of parenting. They are all only suggestions and I'm sure you will come up with many of your own strategies.

When your children are crawling you'd better de-clutter your house! It's really just a safety measure for when you are not right there with them. You will soon find out that coffee tables with sharp corners are a danger. Anything you don't want them to get into in the cupboards (say under the kitchen sink) needs moving, or use those cabinet locks. I know they're a pain, but the alternative is not any less of one.

Here's a quick "tip." When you place toilet paper on a roller make sure to have the loose end come out from the back. Just go do this and you'll see that if a child is hitting the roll it will automatically keep rolling up, NOT down! Look at that! It also saves the puppy from doing the same thing.

There used to be something called a "playpen." I'm not sure what happened to that, but it wasn't a bad idea. Now we have pack 'n plays that are often used for the same thing. In other words, when you have to put a baby down and you want to run to catch that puppy at least a "playpen" will keep them safe in the interim. Always have some favorite toys in there too, of course. How about when you just need two minutes to yourself? Convenient, safe, for short-term use it's a lifesaver.

There are some safety issues that you don't often hear about so here are a couple not on the <u>Tips for Parents</u> list located on the website: www.helpformomcoach.com.

Baby powder is wonderful to keep that little bottom in tip-top shape. It is dangerous if ingested! Breathing in powder can be deadly. Also dangerous is swallowing any Baby Oil. Do not *ever* allow these things within reach of your little darling. When they are tiny and you are always with them at the changing table just keep them up where only you can easily reach. When they become toddlers and still in diapers you know how quick they can be. Be safe, keep all possible dangers out of reach.

Another danger to be aware of are the blinds that have hanging rope to raise and lower a shade, be it material or wood. Place a convenient cup hook way up high to collect the wrapped cord - out of reach. Also, cut the cords and place those plastic caps on the end, just in case a child does get hold of the cord.

Did you get a special baby book before the baby arrived? If you plan on having more than one child, please remember to fill in the second and third with just as much care as you did the first.

The second or third child will know for sure that they were just as important to you. Seriously, your child will think this, it's not just "Oh, for heaven's sake, I JUST haven't had TIME." They will hear, "just not enough time for ME."

Children love to go over and over these books with you and even their friends. So you see, it is something that will be a gift to them for many years and treasured when they leave. Yes, it takes "time" to do this. But like most things in life, if it is important enough we "make" time. What with everything being digital today maybe you don't have to make it such a big chore. Name, date, time of birth, length, color of eyes, hair, etc. It's their concrete reality that they are who they are and who they belong to.

Family is top drawer to us all. So just make it a GREAT memory book. Also a good thing to have in here is some of the "little" things that made you laugh when they were small. Tell the story of when Jimmy took the dog for a walk, only who took whom for a walk? Believe it or not, the stories do run together when you have more than one and some could even be "lost."

Reminder: *Learn and Share More Precious Moments.*

Shared story:

I have a wonderful nephew who writes a letter to his children each birthday. He is saving them (on his computer, a file for each) until they turn 21. It is the sweetest thing to read. He writes about all the things they have done together each year and puts those letters in a story framework. Now that is a gift! You can do this too. Thanks Stephen!

Take a moment to remember some of your own ideas from growing up. What are some ideas that you can come up with that could have a big impact?

Write them down here for safe keeping: _____

_____

_____

_____

_____

_____

_____

How about keeping some ideas the children come up with too! They'll be so proud to be in a "book!" Use your Family Meeting book too. Go to www.helpformomcoach.com for more information.

Reminder: *For a Rainy Day.*

When you are looking for a rainy day project and you have those boxes full of old pictures, let the children learn how to make a scrapbook for themselves of their favorite memories.

Show them how to embellish their work, not just glue them in. Use color, make trim out of colored paper that is cut with pinking shears. Type up what they want said at the bottom of the picture. They (or you) can cut these strips out & paste them in too. These books will be treasured far beyond what you could have imagined and may even be kept right next to The Little Engine That Could.

Here are some samples for **Rainy Day** activities: Scrap booking – self explanatory, but even use computer paper & staple together pages. Or use a hole punch at the top (two holes, 8" apart) & place ribbon through the holes and tie a pretty bow. Coloring/painting – be sure to hang these up, or make a book out of the same as above.

Who could forget fort making – take all the cushions off the furniture in the living room and place them as sides around the coffee table. Or, use a sheet across the tops of the cushions. Sometimes our forts stayed up for days. That is, with several adjustments due to collapses – oops, I mean, redecorating.

Closets are good spots also as is under a desk – sheets to cover the "entrance."

Baking – anything with chocolate, cake, cookies, etc. They can stir at a very young age and licking the spoon is the reward for working sooo hard. Hide & seek. Now this one, you remember how to teach. There's always one who is really good at this and may end up crying because no one ever finds them – even to the point of giving up! Just give a hint to this child to make a "little" noise when they're sure that no one is coming.

So, below is a space for you to add to this list. Just be sure to make it fun! The television does not have to be the only source of entertainment. The magic here is remembering that they want YOU. Spend some time with them at their level instead of on the mobile, or computer. You will be paid back triple, quadrupled in better behavior, listening skills, LOVE.

_____

_____

_____

_____

_____

_____

They do have an inordinate amount of imagination. But, like most things, if they don't exercise that muscle it can be lost. How sad would that be? Ask your kids, "What do you think would be fun? Let's make it up and keep it in our Family Meeting Book so we'll all remember where it is." <u>Family Meeting</u> is under Articles at the same website: www.helpformomcoach.com. Write the children's ideas down here too for the <u>Family Meeting</u> book. Again, they'll feel important <u>and</u> feel special to be in a book! Be sure to put their names beside their ideas:

_____

_____

_____

_____

_____

_____

_____

_____

_____

_____

Their list is longer on purpose!

Reminder: *House Rules.*

Okay, we are now going to get into structure and charting, start young. For those who can't read, place pictures beside the words that you read to them. All children really do love structure. Parents are the ones that may balk at it, but try it and see how it can alleviate stress in your life. Below is a sample for your "House Rules." Have fun with it and include the children in making one up. Make a chart to hang on the refrigerator that targets behaviors that you want to go smoothly and are done every day:

OUR HOUSE RULES

Brush teeth

Wash Face & Hands before every meal

Comb hair

Get dressed – ask for any help

Eat breakfast at the table

Ask to be excused

Clear your place

THANK YOU FOR HELPING ME!

Make up your own list, obviously. Just remember to keep it short.

When you have behaviors that you are trying to change, change the list.

For example, if you are having a bout with biting, No Biting is definitely on the list. Write your own list of House Rules here and give it a week before changing anything. Remember not to target too many behaviors at once. Decorate your chart and make it fun too! Here is space to work on your own:

OUR HOUSE RULES:

_____

_____

_____

_____

_____

_____

_____

Whatever your list is you must convey that to your children by talking about what "house rules" means and that there are consequences for not following them. Young children understand so much more than we give them credit for. They read our faces constantly from early childhood and more often than not have behavior just from that one "look" before the words.

Explain what the consequences are and always keep them the same. I'm assuming that you are not hitting the child here. All psychologists that have written on this subject agree that this is not beneficial in any way.

Another approach takes practice too – doesn't everything? It's called "using your words." The following example is for the child. You as an adult are in charge of yourself. Use your *thinking* skills and change how you speak to your child. In other words (no pun intended!) *think* before you speak, and instead of hitting.

Reminder: *Positive Reinforcement.*

In regard to discipline there are some parents who use quick fixes, like hitting, yelling, or punishing immediately. When we *think* first and decide what it is we want to get out of a given situation, we can also choose to use our words to accomplish the same thing in a gentle, loving manner and have a much bigger impact.

I admit, it's like learning a new language. The best part is, you <u>have</u> all the words already. It's in how you use them that counts.

Always try to come at it from a positive angle. What I mean by that is, say your discipline for biting is "time out." When you send them to "time out" simply repeat, "You've broken our house rule, Jimmy, so you need to *think* about that and when you are ready after your five minutes raise your hand."

Then when you go over to hear the "I'm sorry," you ask for the behavior you <u>want</u>. "Jimmy, thank you for saying I'm sorry, but you also need to say that to Sarah. What were you feeling when you bit Sarah? Is there another way you can let Sarah know that you are angry, or tell her what you want from her? Using our words is always better. Thank you for remembering that. Now next time you can use your words to solve your problem."

This positive reinforcement is difficult to think of on the spot. So be sure to go over different scenarios of the day and HOW you could have made them positive.

Here I would like you to write out a story about something that happened yesterday with your child and how it went. Be specific, write everything you can remember about it, what was said, etc.

_____

_____

_____

_____

_____

_____

_____

_____

_____

_____

What change in language could you make to create *positive* feedback?

_____

_____

_____

_____

_____

_____

_____

_____

Focus on the Behavior that You Want. *What we focus on expands.*

So, do you see that by replaying over and over again the behavior we *don't* want – "Don't bite your sister!" or, "I told you how many times, don't bite your sister! Now go to time out!" It intimates, "go to time out UNTIL you are sorry." Most of us are not sorry because we were mad and the biting took care of our anger. It certainly did, but when we focus on the negative the child learns what NOT to do (by punishment), but not what TO DO instead.

This is all a part of teaching children an inner locus of control. When we have an inner locus of control we go inside to talk to ourselves and understand what the best thing to do is. What is right? Well, those things, believe it or not are taught.

Our children step up to what our expectations are of them. Every time you repeat a comment such as, "Jimmy is the smart one," or, "Jane takes a little time to learn things." That is a pathway that is being ingrained in their minds. Now Jimmy knows he will try his best to be what is expected of him, but if he has a learning disability or not performing in the "A" category he'll feel that he has disappointed his parents, cannot possibly produce and will give up on himself.

"I tried, but I just can't seem to do it. I must be really worthless, especially since they say I'm so great. It's a lie." Now Jane may think to herself, "Oh well, I can't do *that*, so why try?" My own daughter taught me this by explaining to me that, "*You* think I'm that great, but I know I'm not." I was continually boosting her up – or so I thought. In actuality she was not *believing* it because it was not her experience out in the real world. Amazing what we learn from our children.

Every child is perfect in his/her own being. We all come here with something that is unique just to us. When we put parameters on our children we can stunt them and take away their realization of their own magnificence, just as trying to *convince* them of this doesn't work.

Praise for any job well done (good for whatever they are capable of at a given age) shows confidence in them and a "try again" attitude each time. Letting them know that "If at first you don't succeed, try, try again." The perfection is in the *trying* and not giving up.

Reminder: *Unconditional Love At Any Age Is A Plus.*

All children show us **unconditional love** at young ages. Our animals only give unconditional love, no matter how we treat them. There are lessons we could learn by observing them. WE need to be giving unconditional love and only that.

Our children need to know that we *believe* in them. They can and will soar in this lifetime with that kind of trust because they then can find it in themselves. Guide them, nurture them, keep them safe and warm, but most of all show them that you *love* them, *believe* in them (whatever they choose to be in life). Their life is their own, we only have them for a short period of Time. Let's make it the BEST.

Reminder: *List of Strengths to Cheer On.*

So now you have a chance to change what you expect of your child. Instead I'd like you to make a list of your child's strengths. What is it about them that you just cherish, even at a young age? Make this a long list: _____

_____

_____

_____

_____

_____

_____

_____

_____

Add more pages here, if necessary, for each child.

Make a list of HOW you can cheer your child on at whatever stage they are in. If you like, write down the stage of development, or age, whatever is appropriate for you now. Then write about what you are doing to encourage, cheer on, make positive statements of. Again, be specific of the parameters (age) and the *how* you do unconditional love:

Age: _____ What I <u>do</u> to encourage, cheer on, positive statements that I make:

_____

_____

_____

_____

_____

_____

_____

_____

_____

_____

_____

_____

_____

_____

_____

_____

How Do I Encourage My Children?

What Can I do to improve on the list above:

_____

_____

If you need help in any of these areas you can Just Call Your Coach! Go to www.helpformomcoach.com

Reminder: *Teaching moments.*

Another Shared Story:

When my two youngest were traveling with me through town they noticed a young boy on his bicycle to our right on the side of the road that seemed to be swerving a bit. They mentioned it to me and I agreed and gave him a bit more room. Just as we passed him (he was around 12) he "flipped" me off and turned the corner.

I looked in my rearview mirror and knew there was no one behind me, so I backed up. My children knew what I was going to do and they both screamed, "No, Mom, don't talk to him!" I said, "That's exactly what I am going to do. His mother may not be around, but he will hear from me that that behavior is not acceptable!"

I turned the same corner and pulled up in front of him and he stopped. Of course, his mouth was open and totally surprised. I put down my window and said, "That behavior of flipping someone off is not acceptable. I know your mother would not approve if she knew you did that. The reason I'm stopping is also that you must be more careful steering your bicycle. A car cannot always stop as quickly as you and you could have been seriously hurt. Please be careful. Good-bye." And I drove on.

My children were aghast that I would stop and chastise a stranger and, of course, they were embarrassed that I did. So we talked about it and I put it in the context that I certainly would hope that none of my children would do such a thing. Better yet, I would hope that any other mother would stop and say the same thing to them if they did. They saw me do what I speak of with them. It is important to DO the right thing and they witnessed that. It made an impression. One that I may not see or know about in the future, but it enforces the right choices to make in our lives.

We all have teaching moments. Think of one you would like to use from your past.

_____

_____

_____

_____

_____

_____

_____

Teaching moments are like writing a book. We do write on those pages of their experiences.

Reminder: _What's Your Dream? Acceptance._

Make a list here of what you are expecting of your children when they are grown. What dreams do you have for them? Be as descriptive as you can. Go as deep as the dream takes you. Be very detailed, if that is what comes to you. Write on a separate piece of paper if you need it.

_____

_____

_____

_____

_____

_____

_____

_____

_____

_____

_____

_____

_____

That's YOUR dream, what is *theirs*? You say, they don't know yet. But you are going to get them there, right? Is it a dream you had, but couldn't complete because it wasn't the one your parents had for you? Do you really want to repeat this pattern or would you like to set them free to be what they, in their hearts, want to be?

It may not be your dream, but check in as they grow and see what *their* dream is. It's okay. They will make it on their own. You are the parent, not the conductor of the orchestra. We all hear our own music, interpret it in our own unique way. Let *that* BE perfect.

Instead, let us learn how to **accept** one another as we are. Our children often are our teachers. Let's learn from them. If we all accepted each other the way we show up each day, wouldn't that be a different world? Here's Webster's Dictionary explanation: accept v. 1.receive willingly 2.approve 3.agree to 4.believe in - acceptance n.

We think we accept each other as we are, but wait a minute. *Think* about this with regard to your child. Do you accept them as they are? How they show up in this world? Or, do you want to make something else of them? Is it *your* dream for your son to be a doctor. What about your daughter? Well, maybe she could be (whatever you feel is the least that she can be due to her "limitations"). Oh, we could even go farther and ask what we expect of our significant other. What do we "expect" of them? Good question, yes? *Think* about it. If we have expectations we will only get disappointment, anger and frustration.

Our job as parents is to **accept** our children as they show up here. It may not be what we "ordered" (did you really think you could?) but we are responsible to be the adult in their lives who loves, encourages, guides, helps them be the BEST that they can be. This is not to say they have to get the "best" grades, win the swim meet race, or BE anything.

Acceptance means to take them as they are and encourage greatness by teaching them how to "feel" about themselves. Their inner dialogue is what's important. Teach them how to talk to themselves inside. Teach how to check in (with themselves) and in doing so they will not be blaming, whining, or looking *outside* themselves for approval – from you or anyone else.

You're perfect exactly as you are!

In summary, all children show us <u>unconditional</u> love at young ages. Our animals only give <u>unconditional</u> love, no matter how we treat them. WE need to be giving <u>unconditional</u> love and only that. Our children need to know that we *believe* in them. They can and will soar in this lifetime with that kind of trust because they then can find it in themselves.

Guide them, nurture them, keep them safe and warm, but most of all show them that you *love* them, *believe* in them (whatever they choose to be in life). Their life is their own. We only have them for a short period of time. Let's make it the BEST, that is, to *give* the best of ourselves to them.

Find their strengths and drive that one home. You have a list already. If they love art, do projects that you hang all over the house. If they love music, teach them how to make their own CD's with their favorite sound and include their singing. If they love cars, take them to the Auto Show in NYC. Get the point?

I certainly learned this the hard way via four children of my own. The focus for them may even change, especially as a teenager. They are one person one day and another one the next! Who could keep up? Talk to them and find out what fires them up on a continual basis. Don't forget, it is a moving target so keep asking.

Notice and keep track of their passions. What is it that they may have spoken of lately that made their eyes light up? Where were you together when they slipped (thinking to themselves, 'Oops! I forgot, I'm sullen and not interested in anything, or at least I can't let THEM know!') and actually talked to you in an animated way about something? I know you know what I'm going to say here: This list will also show them that it's okay to "change your mind." They may even look at it later in life and say, "I can't believe I wanted to be a Super Hero at age five!" Write them down here for them and hit "Save."

Reminder: *What Is Their Passion?*

_____

_____

_____

_____

_____

_____

_____

_____

Reminder: *Change Rules Into Contracts.*

Teenagers are always another cup of tea. Now the "rules" will become "contracts." Contracts are tools that help enforce House Rules without making them the dreaded "stupid rules" of our house – (that's a teenager speaking). You can contract with your teen for the behaviors that you want. Here are a few that you can post. Don't worry, they all moan and groan over them, but stand tall and be firm. *Remember:* You are not your child's friend.

The following is a sample contract as a guideline for you to make your own. Target whatever is your priority for conduct with your children and be specific about what you are expecting to occur in your home.

Any discussion of the contract is welcome, perhaps at a Family Meeting so everyone involved feels included in this process and agreement. When issues come up you can simply point to the contract and what they *agreed* upon. It often times works like "1, 2, 3 Magic" from when they were little. Below is a contract for our house (make up your own for your <u>Family Meeting</u> book or to be posted on the refrigerator), which we have all agreed upon and will uphold:

CONTRACT FOR THE _____ HOUSE

I will speak the truth

I will be on time

I will help out when asked to, i.e. setting the table

I will be respectful of all who live here

I will ask permission before I borrow the car

I will uphold any laws that are outside this house, i.e.:

No drinking under age

No smoking

No drugs

No driving without a license or under the influence of alcohol

No disrespect shown to those of authority

If I break any of these house rules my consequences will be agreed upon and carried out.

Signatures:

Mom & Dad   Jimmy

_____   _____

_____   Jane

                                             _____

If there is any disagreement, we will discuss it as soon as possible and come up with a solution.

Reminder: *Contracts Are the New Structure.*

We can be so intent on "rules" and "laws" that we miss a step. When our children learn to honor their inner self, sometimes it doesn't match up to the "outer world." Encourage your child to stand up for what he/she believes in. Model this, of course, in your own life.

When your teenager wishes to discuss with you say a question of "fairness," for example, with regard to their teacher at school, give him/her guidance, but encourage him/her to speak his/her own truth. It can be a good topic for discussion that they need to be respectful, but that does not mean not speaking up. You can role play this scenario out so that he/she gets what you are meaning.

Try retelling a story from your past and tell it with appropriate language and then again with inappropriate language. Through your role-playing different scenarios that they may encounter you are encouraging them to speak up for their values. Give them some advice in what words to use to be heard respectfully as well as *being* respectful.

This will also encourage them to come to you for help at a time when they think they have ALL the answers. When we are encouraging and not judgmental of our children we grow their ability to take risks. Risks are stepping stones to growth that we encounter all through life. A leader is one who takes risks. That does not mean uncalculated risks.

Now, you do have to give significant explanation about your choices on the contracts. During the <u>Family Meeting</u> deal with these specifics, especially topics such as *being respectful to all who live here;* no foul language (you can make this a rule too under the contract), speaking when spoken to, no yelling (Mom and Dad, don't forget you are signing this too).

If at all possible it is recommended that the young adults take part in making the choices to put on the contract. Ask them for input. It makes it harder to disagree later when they were the ones to come up with it. You'll be surprised when their minds think of even better ones than you do. This method works on the consequences list as well. When they have thought them up – then they really don't balk. Again, after all, it was their idea!

Because your children have learned to always tell the truth from a very young age this will be ingrained in them. All teenagers lie now and then (you be that model to always tell the truth) and lying is generally to get out of being in trouble for their misguided decisions. We all make mistakes. We all learn from them and move on to do a better job next time.

Your Family Meetings can encapsulate these ideals and is a good place to get your point across. Taking risks is part of growing up. Have you shown courage by taking risks to impart this to your children? We never seem to talk about our struggles. Telling stories about our struggles in life actually make us human to our children. You say, "But I don't want them to do what I did!" The lesson is in the telling of the story. Explaining what bad choices mean and then the gem behind that is: Saying what you learned from it and how you proceeded from there. Here is a shared story of mine to get your own creative juices going.

Shared story:

A friend of mine invited my son to stay for a couple of weeks in the summer. The boys were both around 17 years of age and had gone out to a party at a friend's. They did not come home until very early the next morning and they thought that they could sneak in quietly. Well, Auntie Lora was waiting up in the (dark) kitchen for them.

When the boys tried to deny that they had been drinking she smelled their breath. "I think that's not true." She told them to each get a bucket out of the shed, then return to the kitchen. She gave them each a bit of soap in their buckets and said, "Here, have a sponge and put warm water in the buckets. I expect you to wash all the downstairs windows inside and out and you have until 1PM, <u>not</u> AM! If you do choose *not* to do this task, to my satisfaction, the upstairs windows are next." She left to do errands.

Well, they thought they'd be clever and do the inside first. Unfortunately, when it came to the outside windows it was in the heat of the day! To this day, both boys REMEMBER that summer.

It reminds me of a quote from Vernon Sanders Law (major league baseball player), "Experience is a hard teacher because she gives the test first, the lesson afterwards."

What's your shared story? Write out a story that you could share at a Family Meeting to make it fun. Use a separate piece of paper if needed. You could also print out the result and place it in the <u>Family Meeting book</u>.

My story (Mom): _____

_____

_____

_____

_____

_____

_____

_____

_____

_____

_____

_____

The gem I learned is: _____

_____

_____

_____

_____

_____

_____

_____

My story (Dad): _____

_____

_____

_____

_____

_____

_____

_____

_____

_____

_____

_____

_____

The gem I learned is: _____

_____

_____

_____

_____

_____

_____

_____

Reminder: *How to Implement the Contract.*

Sharing personalizes us to our children. In other words, we need to be more willing to show our vulnerabilities, our mistakes, but more importantly how we dealt with them.

It also means that we need to be more human than parent to them as they move into adulthood. When we only see our parents as authoritative, penalizing, and controlling, it leaves us in a never-never land where there is no appreciation for who "we" are. The person inside the parent is our true self. When we stay a "parent" *only*, our children come home to visit and revert back to the five year old or the 15 year old.

Growing up our relationships with our children (allowing us both to be adults) takes deliberate intention and also enables us to "let them go."

To 'let go' is a metaphor for allowing our children to be who they are in their true self. We are not the choreographer of their lives, they are. In learning to let them go we have to trust that they have a path to follow. When they come to us for guidance we can give an opinion, but never have an invested interest in the outcome.

When we raise our children with strong values of faith (whatever your faith may be) we teach them that their inner strength comes not from us as parents, but from their inner core.

Using integrity as a guide is important. We are going to have challenges in life. It is most of what life is made up of, right? It's not what happens in life that matters, it is how you deal with it that counts. Integrity is an illusive term for young people. We find in Webster's Dictionary the definition says: integrity n. 1.honesty, sincerity, etc, 2.wholeness.

In sharing stories about our own lives, we can enumerate to our children what integrity is. If they see that no matter how bad the circumstances were, we just picked ourselves up, corrected what we could, apologized when necessary and moved on with our heads held high, they can believe that they can too. Not only that they can, but more importantly, how to do it. Do you have a story to share now?

Your Story.

(Mom):_____

_____

_____

_____

_____

_____

_____

_____

_____

_____

_____

_____

_____

_____

_____

_____

_____

_____

_____

_____

(Dad): _____

_____

_____

_____

_____

_____

_____

_____

_____

_____

_____

_____

_____

_____

_____

_____

_____

_____

_____

Whatever the infraction is and whatever the consequence is YOU MAY NOT CHANGE YOUR MIND ONCE IT IS AGREED. Just like when they were "little" you may have thought to yourself, "Well, it has been two days and he's behaved pretty well. I could cut it down a bit…" DON'T! The one who will "pay" is Y O U.

To back down or change the consequence, shows the teenager that he can still manipulate you into what he wants. All kids want out of the consequence, of course. But when you allow this (the change of the consequence) you lose credibility in their eyes. You have now become putty in their hands. You CAN be manipulated, just like when they were "little."

The "rules" remember have not changed, just the word "contract." We tend to think things are different because they are older. Just remember to stand firm, and be the parent. Stick to the rules. All the techniques you learned when they were younger still apply.

Spend some time discussing possible infractions and what the consequences may be. Remember to ask the children for a list as well. Often, they will come up with much better consequences than we ever could. They will not balk as much because they have agreed and even thought them up themselves. Let's be inventive and make a list of infractions and consequences. Sit and talk about them and see what comes up for you. What part of the contract is broken, explain:

_____

_____

_____

_____

_____

_____

_____

_____

What is the consequence?: _____

_____

_____

_____

_____

_____

_____

_____

_____

Are you being a "friend" to your child? Are you afraid they will not *like* you? You are not their friend. At this time in their life they still NEED a PARENT. YOU ARE IT! They will not get any lessons, if you are trying to be a friend.

So BE the parent. That docile "little one" is no longer inhabiting this body in front of you. The body looks like a full grown adult, but don't be fooled. Take charge, **Remember**: You do not have to "lose it" to make your point. The fewer words spoken, the better. Then walk away.

State your point but don't belabor it when they say nothing. For some reason when as parents we do not hear something in return (normally called a conversation) we repeat ourselves.

There was a birthday card I bought for my 20 year old son and it said on the outside: HAPPY BIRTHDAY, HAPPY BIRTHDAY, HAPPY BIRTHDAY! Then when you open it up it said, "Sorry, I can't seem to get out of the habit of repeating myself at least three times!"

You will laugh at this too at some point. They have heard you the first time. And if they act otherwise, what are the consequences? Whatever it is, it is *theirs*, right? Don't jump in to save them from any discomfort for there in lie the nuggets of learning.

Let's correlate two different scenarios from two different time slots:

Your five year old leaves his/her tricycle out in the driveway at the end of the day. You warned him/her that it needs to be put away so Daddy doesn't inadvertently drive over it when he gets home. Daddy arrives home and comes in the driveway and can't miss the tricycle, crunch!

Of course we have tears and Daddy apologizes for not seeing it, etc. What do you do? I know a lot of us would have told the child: "Don't cry, Daddy didn't <u>mean</u> to crush your tricycle! We'll go get a new one tomorrow, but you must remember to put your tricycle away, like I told you."

What if the consequence was: "Jimmy, I know you're upset that Daddy crushed your tricycle. It was in a place that he could not avoid hitting it when he comes in the driveway. If you save your allowance we can replace the tricycle, but what do you need to remember?"

Your 16 year old is going out to the store to run an errand for you. You gently ask if he has his license with him. "Yeah, of course!" He takes a bit longer than you'd expect and returns home with a Warning from a nice policeman (who followed him home). "Mom! Where's my license?! I have to show the officer to prove that I have one and then he'll just give me a Warning." Mom: "Well that is nice of the officer. I have no idea where your license is. Where do you keep it?"

Can you see any similarity? The five year old will learn and NEVER leave his tricycle in the driveway again because it cost him dearly. First he did not have one for a couple of weeks. Also, his allowance needed to go towards it and that hurt. The 16 year old got the real lesson from outside authority. If you are learning here, you did not help him find his license, and you did <u>not</u> go outside to speak to the officer. HE will not forget his license again. He also learned the responsibility of his actions were his alone.

The consequences are the same. ACTIONS=CONSEQUENCES

If you can remember this one sentence and apply it often you will be *thinking* on a regular basis and stay conscious (present) in each day: **Thoughts Become Manifest**.

What we *think* gives us our *feelings*, and that gives us the *behavior*, that becomes the *result*. Our THOUGHTS are the creation of our own reality. What about the saying, "Be careful what you wish for?" It sounds more empowering now doesn't it? Just *Think* about your thoughts.

Thank you for taking the time to read this. I hope that it has been beneficial to you and has given you some insights and ideas into your own parenting. If you ever need a hand with brainstorming your own plan or just need a few moments for yourself,

Just Call Your Coach… www.helpformomcoach.com